You DESERVE
a great flight!

Help Me Fly

Relaxed & Safe From Takeoff To Touchdown

Natalie Windsor

Illustrations by
Joe Azar

EnterActing Media
LOS ANGELES

ABOUT THE AUTHOR

You can hear **Natalie Windsor** on the radio across the USA as a correspondent for Associated Press Radio Network. But what she does in her spare time would fry any couch potato: she's written travel books; sung professionally in clubs, religious settings of many denominations, and Dodger Stadium; recorded books on World War II, Buddhism and gene splicing for the Library of Congress Talking Book Program, and is oddly proud of being a past national president of the (sadly) now defunct Committee to End Pay Toilets in America (CEPTIA).

Published by EnterActing Media
A division of Tridactic, Inc.
2029 Verdugo Blvd., Suite 212 • Montrose CA 91020
Find us online at *helpmefly.net*

Distribution to the book trade in the United States: Plymouth Press (800) 350-1007

ISBN 0-9715813-6-3

For information on quantity discounts and custom imprintings for sales promotions, premiums, fundraising or education, please contact EnterActing Media.

Manufactured in the United States of America

10   9   8   7   6   5   4   3   2   1

To
my loved ones
and yours, who give us
the motivation and bravery
to conquer the skies—
and anything else
between us.

To Shoshana, Rich & Joe—
with love, gratitude and admiration.

Acknowledgments
Many thanks to the people who lent their knowledge and wisdom to this book: Jill Bradley, PT; Barry Brayer, FAA; Elly Brekke, FAA; Joel Chineson; Bill Hoffer, National Weather Service; Agnes J. Huff, CEO, ágnes huff communications group, llc; Dr. Marina Biallo; Pat Jorgenson, U.S. Geological Survey; Timothy Kelly, USDOT; Arthur Lampel, JD; Bob Matthews, manager of safety promotion, FAA; David Melancon, Association of Flight Attendants; Ilan Migdali, L. Ac; Prof. Peter Monkewitz, UCLA Department of Mechanical & Aerospace Engineering; Dr. Robert Murphy, DDS; Jon A. Pace, hypnotherapist; Fred Pelzman, Community & Consumer Liaison Division, FAA; Victor J. Gill, director, Public Affairs and Communications, Burbank Glendale Pasadena Airport Authority; Wendy Perrin, *Condé Nast Traveler*; Emily Porter, ASTA; Jani Nayar, Society for the Advancement of Travel for the Handicapped; Sue Riemer; Dr. Gary Bellack; Dr. Lyle Kurtz; Chris English; Steve Spar; Patrick Walsh; Lisa Beezley; and the many flight attendants, reservation agents, frequent flyers and nervous passengers interviewed for this book. May all your flights be comfortable, safe and on time.

Cover design by Ken Niles

Foreword

Flying in the New Age of Air Travel

Let's not kid ourselves. Air travel may never again be as simple as it once was. But that's not necessarily entirely bad: we'll trade some hassles for increased security. This still gives us all the advantages of covering great distances in relatively short time.

I once knew a man who referred to his Piper Cherokee as a time machine. He described it as "the invention that lets me have lunch in Chicago and sleep at home in

my own bed in Cleveland the same night."
Air travel gives us the opportunity to kiss
Grandma again, to see Hawaii's volcanoes and Alaska's glaciers, to climb Masada and walk the Stations of the Cross—emotions and adventures our great-grandparents couldn't even imagine.

You are not only getting where you want to go—you are showing the world you will not be stopped.

Air travel these days may require more careful planning and packing, more delays and inconvenience, and more faith in the companies and people pledged to keep us safe. But it's also the shortest distance between loved ones and points of personal importance. Focusing on what we gain by it, rather than on what we

worry about, gives us more of the benefits and fewer of the fears.

Whether you draw your strength from sheer need, safety statistics or a Higher Power, know that you are not only getting where you want to go—you're showing the world you will not be stopped.

So, if you're traveling on business—close a big deal. On vacation—go for the gusto. Visiting loved ones—hug someone special. And have a good trip!

P.S. If you have a personal tip or mantra that gets you more happily through a flight—or could help others—please email me at *natalie@helpmefly.net* I'd love to hear from you.

What Would YOU Like To Know?

Table of
Contents

How fortunate we are to have the ability to travel!

150 years ago people packed their lives into covered wagons and spent months riding over rugged trails, constantly facing danger, hardship and disease.

100 years ago people loaded their lives into steamer trunks deep in the holds of crowded ships. The long weeks at sea meant many would never go back to their homelands again.

60 years ago air travel was available only to the very rich and the very brave. Early propeller planes bounced adventurers across unfriendly skies. Crossing the USA took long dusty days of driving or riding; loved ones stationed a thousand miles away got postcards and packages, not visits.

Today we can kiss loved ones goodbye in the morning—visit faraway cities—and return home in time to kiss them good-night. Air travel gives us control over our time and our world.

We are truly empowered to be able to fly.

How Are You Doing Right Now?

How'd you like
to do better?

Experts say as many as 40 percent of adult Americans admit to being scared of flying, with another 10 percent refusing to get on a plane at all. Fear keeps people from attending loved ones' weddings, enjoying Hawaii's tropical tranquility, or accepting higher-paying jobs that require air travel.

Experts also say the more you learn about the safety of modern aircraft, how it lifts off and lands, and what its noises mean, the more you can relax.

Taking your thoughts to where YOU want them to go helps you relax, too. And learning a few simple breathing techniques lets you stay calm and composed. Simply put, your mind needs to be elsewhere.

This isn't about you. Somebody *really* wants to see you—that's why you're on the plane, right? Close your eyes and see their face, thrilled and surprised and so very glad you went to the effort of traveling. This trip isn't about you—see it for the joy or gift or obligation met, and what it means to the somebody you're flying for.

Stay positive. Experts say your mind focuses on the nouns, regardless of what else is in the sentence. That is, "Don't think about pink elephants," is retained as "pink elephants." That defeats your purpose. So if you're going to talk to yourself, remind yourself of the times you have been brave —and what you won or attained as a result.

Heat up your seat time. Play a mental video of the romantic adventure you want to have after you arrive—or replay your all-time best romantic adventure. (For the sake of those around you, try not to moan!)

Are you anxious right now?

- Feelings don't make it real. Your discomfort is not a sign of danger.

- Acknowledge and accept that you are a passenger, and your only job is to make yourself comfortable. That's the only part of the situation you need to control.

- Turn the page and keep reading.

- Try the breathing exercises on page 30.

- Take a Mental Field Trip on page 36.

- Read about airplane noises on page 108.

- Tell a flight attendant if you're nervous, so you don't have to hide your anxiety for the entire flight.

- After you land, look into treatment options: support groups, ease-of-flying seminars, books and tapes, or private therapy.

Are you hyperventilating? When you involuntarily breathe too fast, the carbon dioxide level in your blood can drop too low. This can also bring on a racing heart; lightheadedness; the feeling that you can't get enough air; or numbness or tingling in your hands, feet, or around your mouth. These are just temporary symptoms.

Look for the airsickness bag in the seat-pocket in front of you. Hold it over your nose and mouth and slowly breathe in and out. This will help bring the amount of carbon dioxide in your blood back to normal. If you need to, continue till you feel better.

If you think you may hyperventilate, ask your seatmate to do you a favor and mention if you're starting to breathe too fast.

If you realize you're breathing too fast, or feel any of the symptoms above, try the slow breathing exercises on pages 30-35.

A Little Viagra
For The Soul

"Courage is contagious.
When a brave man takes
a stand, the spines of
others are often stiffened."

—Billy Graham

You have so much more power than you know—and you're more of a leader than you realize. The feelings you carry radiate from your voice, your expressions and your gestures—what Californians call your "vibe."

When you're angry, glad or frightened, other people sense it and often catch your vibe. Dogs aren't the only ones who can smell fear.

What does this mean to you? You have a hundred more reasons than you think to behave well. Every timid soul, child or senior citizen around you will take your subconscious cue.

Behaving with intelligent awareness instead of twitchy panic will do two things:

1. It will make the people around you more comfortable and confident, and

2. It will make you much more comfortable inside your own skin.

It's fine to have a gap between how you feel and how you behave. The important thing is to recognize this gap and *still* behave well...if just for the sake of that kid across the aisle.

Give Yourself A Mental Dress Rehearsal

What you need,
before you need it —
so all your travel reflexes
are second nature.

HelpMeFly.net 21

You know the best way to keep it from raining, don't you? When you're carrying an umbrella, you never seem to have to use it. That's why you deserve a mental dress rehearsal: so your reactions, reflexes and decisions will come so easily, that of course, you'll never need to use them.

Pack smart. Sift through your carry-on for the innocent cuticle scissors or nail file tucked inside your toiletry kit—and move them into that suitcase you plan to check.

Be aware. No gliding through the airport on autopilot. Pay attention.

It's not tattling. Report unusual activity. If you see anything in the airport or on the plane that seems odd or inappropriate, tell somebody in authority.

Good or bad—don't assume. Outfits and hair color don't mean a thing when it comes to picking good guys. If your gut says someone's behavior is unusual, don't hesitate to report it. But don't be misled. Report your observations—not your prejudices.

No kidding. Innocent jokes and inappropriate comments are taken very

More Mental Dress Rehearsals

seriously, and can land you in an interrogation room rather than your intended destination. Keep your wiseacre comments to yourself—especially while answering security questions.

Wear your seatbelt. That snug hug around the hips provides extra protection from turbulence—no extra charge! Keep wearing it even if they turn off the seatbelt light.

Listen up! The flight attendants aren't giving those safety demonstrations to amuse themselves. Being indifferent means you lose important information. Being disrespectful means the person in the seat next to you loses, too.

Know your plane. As soon as you buckle up, scope out the cabin. Look for the row of lights on the floor designed to make a dark cabin safer. Count how many rows you are from the closest door, and who's sitting in the seats around you who might need your help.

Respect the electronics rules.
Remember: cell phones, pagers and other cordless electronics may be used until the plane's doors are closed. Rules vary around the world—if the flight attendants don't tell you, ask.

You're happier when you're rehearsed.
Knowing what you want to do before you need to do it gives you enormous power and confidence. Make a mental note now which one phone call would inform and assist the most. If you ever need the FBI, call (202) 324-3000—or call 911 from any phone anywhere in the United States.

You're not Schwarzenegger. If you are ever in a dangerous situation, pulling an *Ah-nold* and taking solo action is incredibly stupid. It is almost always better to share the information with some-one in authority. Unless you are working in concert with people who are informed and trained, you're much more likely to make it worse than to make it better.

You're Not Alone

Make a 4-hour friend

If you're flying alone, give yourself some-one to be brave for. Hold in your heart and mind someone whom you want to make proud of you.

Better yet—in most cases—introduce your-self to the person sitting right next to you. You're not committing to a cross-country heartfelt confession session, you're just putting a first name to that face and making each other real people worth keeping up appearances for.

Knowing even one fact about your seat-mate can help you bolster each other, even as you ignore each other. Because—face it—you're in this thing together for the next few hours.

Hurry Up
And Wait

Your biggest challenge at the airport may well be boredom. Arriving two hours early may leave you checked in and ready to go, with *waaaay* too much time on your hands.

Don't be lulled by leadtime. You can easily miss that last boarding call if you're not paying attention. You only have 'plenty of time' if you're paying attention to its passage.

Stay away from alcohol and sleep-inducing high-fat snacks. If your mystery novel is absorbing, make a habit of looking up after each two-page spread. Keep track of your time, your surroundings, and your bag or purse—it's safest between your feet.

Don't be crazed by the kids. If you're traveling with youngsters, remember that they'll have up to two hours of 'amuse yourself quietly' time before they get on the plane for the 'strap-me-in-for-a-really-long time-out.' Pack a busy-bag full of varied snacks, crayons and toys.

Flying With Kids

How to pack all the facts,
reassurance and hugs
they'll need.

Traveling with kids wasn't so easy even *before* September 11th. What can you say to them now to make it a less fearful experience? The answer is, it's probably more important what you DON'T say.

Your children take their cues from you and the behavior you model. And what you say to your children is probably less important than *listening to what they say to you.*

Letting them air their feelings and fears shows where you need to offer truthful reassurance. For instance, some children misunderstood the replays of the news footage of 9/11: they thought dozens of planes had hit dozens of buildings, and the U.S. was under full-scale attack.

Just remember that facts go only so far toward amending feelings. Helping channel emotions is tougher—especially if you don't have the words yet to explain it to yourself.

Expect to be asked the same questions over and over, even though you think you've answered them already; and respond each time as though it were new.

Children need a lot of reassurance that they're safe, and that you'll be there for them. They also need to know that authorities are doing everything they can to protect us. Remind them that our job is to keep doing what we're supposed to do, and stay in contact with each other a little more than usual.

In short, treat questions about terrorism the same way you'd treat questions about sex: keep your answers short and simple, address only the questions asked, and volunteer no new information that would raise new questions. This will require your patience, but isn't your child worth that? Because while you can't absolutely guarantee bad things won't happen, you also don't want your children to live their lives in fear.

And don't forget the power of a hug. It carries no facts, just consolation and love.

Secrets To Staying Calm & Relaxed

From acupressure
to breathing
to Yabba Dabba

If You Feel Panicky Right Now

Breathe In.
Count to three.

Breathe Out.
Count to three.

Breathe and Count.

Breathe and Count.

Do this over and over until it
makes a rhythm and your
heartbeat is more normal.

If you can, read on. If not,
just keep breathing and counting—
that's just fine.

If you like, someone can read
this to you, slowly, as you are
ready for each section.

You Are In Control

Panic attacks are really about
feeling in control.

YOU ARE IN CONTROL.

More than it feels like, you are.

Feel your back against the seat.

Feel your feet on the floor,
and your arms on the armrests.

You are on a journey you planned,
to a destination YOU chose.
This is very good.

You are close to trained people who
will help you if you need it.

BREATHE IN. Count to three.

BREATHE OUT.

THIS MOMENT WILL PASS.

Put your hands on the edges of the
armrests, and squeeze as tight as
you like; then deliberately release
and rest. No one will notice. You
can send your feelings into the seat
arms: press, count to three and
release, press, count to three and
release. Make the rhythm the same
as your breathing.

You Are Safe, And Doing Better

Every time you breathe out,
send a bit of tension out with
the tide of your breath.

Every time you count to three,
use that count to send the
tension into the outgoing
breath. Layer it on the stream of
air, just like buttering a piece of
bread, and send it out of you.

As long as you sit still and quiet
in your seat, no one will notice.

Breathe in, count to three,
breathe a little tension out.

If you want to, call the
attendant. They are trained to
assist you, and they will be
there for you if you need them.

THIS MOMENT WILL PASS.

BREATHE IN,
COUNT TO THREE.

BREATHE THE FEELINGS OUT.

Mental Field Trips

Take a breather with this
guided tour of your
mental landscape.

Mental field trip guidelines

Hypnotherapists use guided visualizations for everything from improving golf games to calming fears. The mind doesn't distinguish between reality and imagination when it comes to physical reaction. That's why visualizing a bright yellow juicy sour lemon touching your tongue can actually make you salivate—vivid thoughts FEEL real to your mind. *See?*

These visualizations can assist your flexibility on a long flight, and even keep your feet from swelling. Read through one mental field trip until you have the gist of it, then put down the book and take your tour.

Mental Field Trip #1

Sit up straight, legs uncrossed, feet flat on the floor, and close your eyes. In your mind, see a place where you walk—your favorite park, the smooth marble floors of a well-lit shopping mall, the long halls at work...any place you feel comfortable.

Put yourself in that setting, ready to walk, and begin.

Follow a path that pleases you: look at the flowers and watch the dogs playing, scope out the shops with the best bargains, see which co-workers' doors are open, and what each is doing in the offices. Internally narrate the tour to yourself or to a walking buddy (wanna stroll with Einstein or Madonna? It's your visualization—have it any way you want it!). Feel your tendons stretching and your ankles working. Feel your calf muscles elongating to accommodate slight slopes, and see yourself adjusting your speed and stride as you walk.

Rehearsing in your mind has total psychological validity, and can keep you from stiffening up in your seat. Side effects from a "walk" like this can include a clearer head and a better frame of mind.

Mental Field Trip #2

Close your eyes and visualize your feet and legs in your mind's eye. See the skin, the scars, the beauty marks, the...*hey!* Make sure these are YOUR legs!

Now, in your mind, give yourself a foot massage. Start with your toes on one foot. Rub the ball of your foot, the instep, the heel, the inside and outside of your ankle. Imagine your hands applying gentle pressure to the top and bottom of your foot, then up the calf. Feel the sensations of what you "see" your hands doing. Now, do the other foot.

Make sure your massage begins at the toes and works up your leg. Take three minutes to imagine this each hour, or as often as you like. A mental foot massage can actually keep feet from swelling during the flight. And better yet: it's free!

Mental Field
Trip #3

Relax your head into the cushion. Untense your muscles. Close your eyes. Now imagine you're sitting next to Babe Ruth—and he's buying *you* a beer. He's got a lot of questions, you see, and you seem to know about baseball.

"What's this nonsense about designated hitters?" he sniffs. "Who is Maris? Sosa? McGuire? Bonds?" he asks. "And who the hell is John Rocker?"

Go ahead. Fill him in. Explain why the Giants and Dodgers weren't in the last subway series. Tell him what's up with the price of hot dogs in the stadium he built. And if you've got the nerve, tell him how many millions he would've earned if he played in the majors this year.

Your turn. Ask what it was like to hit three homers in one World Series game. Twice. How it felt to bat .847 in 1920 (score points by telling him his slugging record has *never* been broken.) And since it's mostly just guys reading this far, ask him about his storied exploits *off* the field, too. His juicy tales of wine, women and song could take you all the way to the landing announcement!

On-The-Spot Remedies

Away from your medicine cabinet, any ache can be agony. A couple of trade secrets can go a long way towards easing discomforts in the privacy of your seat.

ACUPRESSURE
Full-Court Press Against Pain

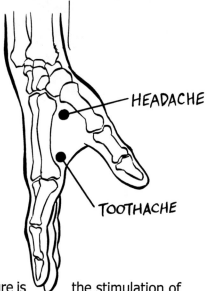

HEADACHE

TOOTHACHE

Acupressure is the stimulation of specific points along your body's energy channels, and it works whether you believe in it or not. Ask the billions of Chinese who have used it for thousands of years. Simply trying it uses your time constructively—it costs nothing, requires no equipment and creates no side effects. You have nothing to lose but your pain.

Cure Your Headache

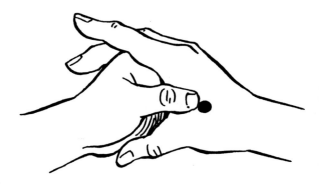

There's an acupressure point named Hegu (the Yuan-Source point, if you're into Oriental medicine trivia) on the fleshy part of your hand, between your thumb and forefinger. To find it, move your left thumb up into the 'V' between the bones of your right thumb and right forefinger, as far up as it will go without hitting the bone. Press on that spot—not hard enough to hurt—just medium pressure until the headache goes away. To assist the healing further, close your eyes and breathe deeply.

Relieve Your Toothache

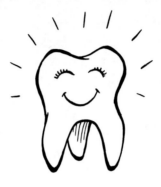

Serious dental problems may feel worse on a plane. You could be surprised by a cavity you didn't know you had, or a chronic twinge that turns out to be an excruciating abscess after takeoff. It's a good idea not to fly within 12 hours of dental work.

Find Sanjian, the Shu-Stream point, by first finding the headache point with your thumb, and then backing off half-way along the forefinger bone. When you make a loose fist, the toothache point is right next to the end of the bone in your hand that connects with your forefinger. Press forcefully until the pain begins to diminish. Closing your eyes, clearing your mind and breathing deeply will assist this process.

Keeping Lunch

If you're having a little trouble catching a full breath, or your stomach is uneasy, try this. Feel for the acupressure point above your inner wrist, two fingers' width up your arm above the crease. Press this as though you were taking a pulse. Close your eyes, breathe deeply and focus on the air cleansing your system as it goes in and out of your lungs.

An alternative stomach-settling point can be found on the crease of your inner elbow. Roll up your sleeve and bend your arm slightly to see the crease, and feel the tendon in the middle of the bend. This point is on the inner side of the tendon, just below where your biceps muscle begins. Press this point as hard as is comfortable, close your eyes, breathe deeply and focus on your breath going in and out.

These two points will regulate your heartbeat, calm your stomach and release the tension in your elbows, arms and shoulders. The elbow-point can also relieve dry-mouth.

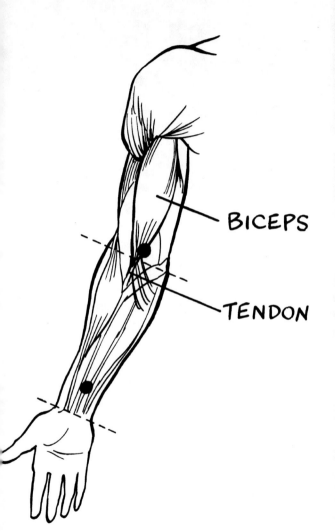

BICEPS

TENDON

Quick Pick-Me-Ups

Try these feel-good ideas from frequent flyers—and the people who serve them:

+ Wear your most comfortable shoes. If you must wear dress shoes, remove them—feet and ankles swell during long periods of inactivity. Carry a plastic shoehorn to help put them back on.

+ Loosen ties, belts and other restrictive clothing. Ask your flight attendant for pillows—place one behind your head and one supporting your lower back.

+ In-flight temperatures can vary considerably. Dress in layers of natural fabrics —a light sweater or jacket could come in handy.

+ Drink lots of bottled water or juice to counteract dehydration. Avoid gassy carbonated drinks (no dogs to blame). Go easy on coffee and alcohol—they only dehydrate you more.

+ Since the air in the plane is dry, you'll

feel better wearing glasses instead of contact lenses.

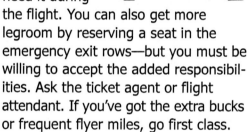

✈ Give yourself lots of room to stretch your legs. Put your carry-on in the overhead bin if you won't need it during the flight. You can also get more legroom by reserving a seat in the emergency exit rows—but you must be willing to accept the added responsibilities. Ask the ticket agent or flight attendant. If you've got the extra bucks or frequent flyer miles, go first class.

✈ Relieve the strain on your back. Keep your knees higher than your hips by putting a briefcase or small carry-on under your feet.

✈ Get some shut-eye. Use an eye shade if necessary. Bring an inflatable U-shaped travel pillow for your neck. For sleeping upright, it works like a dream!

✈ Get up and walk to the lavatory. Try the stretching exercises on page 56.

Carry-On Mood Boosters

Snack Time. Airlines don't feed you like they used to, so bring your own favorite foods. Good snacks to pack: unsalted nuts, dried or fresh fruits, pre-sliced veggies, and low-fat mini-cheeses sealed in wax.

Aprés snacks. A toothbrush and minty toothpaste are a cheap, easy way to reassert your sense of well-being, as well as de-fur your mouth.

Overcome dry airplane air. Sample-sized bottles of unscented hand lotion and saline nasal spray will keep you comfortable. Bring bottled water, or buy a bottle in the airport.

Bring "home" with you. Carry your favorite calming teabags—and ask the flight attendant for hot water.

Don't *pooh-pooh* aroma therapy. A small sachet or familiar-smelling object can be very calming.

Write a letter. Certain things are more personal in your own handwriting than in an email. Here's your chance.

I *vant* to be alone. Very dark sunglasses are great for snoozing. People may think you're a movie star.

Bedroom slippers. Unless you're being followed by paparazzi, wear slippers once you're seated. Changing your heel height can give you a new attitude.

Van Cliburn or Van Morrison? Bring a few hours' worth of soothing music on a portable player—and let your headsets transport you to your destination.

Whaa? I Can't Hear You...

How to Unstuff Your Ears

As the plane begins to land, the resulting changes in air pressure can wreak havoc on your eardrums. Even though the cabin is pressurized, your ears may feel stuffy or painful, and regular noises may not sound as loud for a little while.

At the first sign of discomfort, try these techniques, especially if you're flying with a bad cold. If at first you don't succeed, try a different one:

Chew gum or suck candy. The constant motion of the jaw and continued swallowing can help relieve the pressure.

Take a decongestant. If you have a cold, descent can be tougher on your ears and sinuses. Take a decongestant or nasal spray so its effects are timed to coincide with takeoff and landing.

Yawn. Force yourself. Then keep yawning.

Pinch your nose. Now close your lips, hold your breath and swallow hard. Do it again.

Take a small breath. Pinch your nose. Now very gently try to blow out through your nose till your ears pop. (Note: doctors advise not to use this technique if you have a cold, upper-respiratory tract infection, or heart problems.)

Feed your infant during descent. This will reduce pressure in your baby's ears. You can also use a pacifier.

Keep trying. If your ears still aren't clear after landing, try these techniques a few more times. If stuffiness or pain continue, see a physician.

In-Seat S-t-r-e-t-c-h-i-n-g

Even seasoned couch potatoes have trouble sitting for long flights. There's no TV to stare at, no refrigerator to go to, and not even a couch to lie down on.

But there is one way to limber up while you relieve the boredom and stiffness of a long flight: *stretch*. It'll get your blood circulating, and help you feel invigorated, especially after napping.

Here's how: Remember to go slow and easy—small movements work just fine. Your goal is gentle stretching, not grunts, flailing or breaking a sweat.

Take a short walk through the plane every couple of hours, too. Try taking the longer route to the lavatory, and then do a few knee bends outside the door.

You can do the following exercises right in your seat. If your seatmates look puzzled, do them a favor: show them this book so they can flex out, too!

The Yabba Dabba II

Pretend you're driving the Flintstones' car and 'jog' the plane across Bedrock.

Then rotate your feet at the ankles, first clockwise, then counterclockwise. Do the same with your wrists.

The "Let's Neck"

Keeping your shoulders down, turn your head to the right, and stretch ear-to-shoulder. Repeat on the left side.

Then, with the same motion, stretch your *chin* over your right shoulder. Repeat on left side.

The Bun Warmer

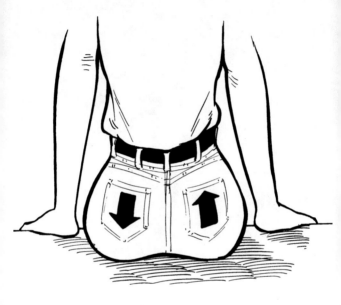

Keep the beat with your cheeks.
Alternately tense and relax your right and
left gluteus maximus muscles, in time
with the music on the headset.

The "I Dunno"

Shrug, as if someone just asked if you
know the square root of 873. Bring your
shoulders up to your ears, and then lower
them as far as they'll go. Feels good,
huh? So do it again.

The Annoyer

Clasp your hands behind your head, and pull your elbows back toward the seat, squeezing your shoulder blades closer together. Relax and repeat.

Kicking Jet Lag

Fatigue. Insomnia. Disorientation. Loss of appetite. No, it's not love, it's jet lag.

You can get it when you fly across several time zones, and your body rhythms need a few days—or weeks—to catch up. Jet lag is normal, but it's distressing when you're at an 8 a.m. breakfast meeting and your brain insists you should still be asleep.

How to beat the body-clock blues

The good news is that you won't be jet lagged when you fly north or south—just tired. But jet lag can compound your flying fatigue on any east-west flight that crosses time zones—even one.

Doctors and sleep specialists are still learning better ways to beat jet lag so you can arrive feeling refreshed. There are a number of remedies available now, from diet adjustment to sunlight therapy, and they may or may not work for you. Your travel agent or a website could point you in the right direction, but the best advice will come from your physician. The idea is to trick your body into resetting its internal clock. Here are a few tips to get you started:

✈ Skip caffeine the day of your flight, and eat lightly if at all while you're in the air.

✈ Avoid all alcohol. Drink lots of bottled water and juice.

✈ Book your flight later in the day so you can sleep on the plane and arrive after dark.

✈ At your destination, try to remain awake until 11 o'clock that evening—without napping in between.

✈ To avoid napping when your body is craving sleep, go out into the sunlight and take a walk.

✈ Set your watch for your destination as soon as you board the plane, and do what the locals do. If it's suppertime, eat a light supper, even if your body says it's bedtime.

✈ Repeat this procedure when you return home.

✈ Consult your physician if you plan to take any jet lag medication.

✈ If you take any medications with timed doses (antibiotics, insulin, birth control pills, etc.) consult your physician about timing changes *before* you go.

✈ Try not to make any major decisions for at least 24 hours after landing—you won't be at your best.

Confident Flying

Tips from the pros
to help you fly
more safely and easily.

Captain Wrightway's FLIGHT PREP

Things can change so quickly now, the Captain advises you ask these questions BEFORE you leave for the airport.

Ask your AIRLINE:

✈ Is my flight leaving on schedule?

✈ Any luggage and carry-on restrictions: size, weight, number of bags and odd-size containers?

✈ Do I need any special documentation for an e-ticket?

Ask your AIRPORT(S):

✈ What are the current arrangements for parking and curbside access?

✈ For early departures, what time does the airport open?

✈ Where's the best place to meet the people I'm flying to see?

For all connecting airline and airport information: *www.helpmefly.net*

In Advance

✈ Security rules are still evolving—call or visit the websites of your airline and departure and arrival airports to find out what to expect.

✈ Make your reservations in the exact same name that appears on your photo ID. If your name has recently changed due to marriage, bring a copy of your marriage certificate.

✈ Carry-ons are now limited to one bag that will fit under an airplane seat—call your airline to ask what that means in inches. You're also allowed one small personal item such as a purse, briefcase, laptop or backpack.

✈ If your carry-on is considered too big when you arrive at the gate, plan to check it there. Remove all valuables, medications and fragile items.

✈ Never pack these items in any checked bag: money, passport, keys, eyeglasses, camera, jewelry, medicine, tickets or irreplaceable items.

✈ Always pack any personal things you'll need for 48 hours in your carry-on.

✈ Pack expecting that your bags will be opened and thoroughly examined by security personnel. Put small items into clear zip-close plastic bags. Don't overstuff your suitcases.

✈ Some innocent everyday toiletries can be dangerous on airplanes, and the airlines define hazardous items broadly. Don't pack aerosols like hairsprays, cigarette lighters and loose matches in luggage you plan to check. Also, anything corrosive, flammable or affected by air pressure (like diver's tanks) need special transport. Call ahead for information.

✈ If you pack wrapped gifts in your carry-on, you may have to unwrap them at the security checkpoint. Put wrapped gifts in your checked luggage, or wrap gifts after you arrive.

✈ Attach two luggage tags to each bag with the address and phone number of your business or your destination— never your home. That billboards your absence to burglars.

✈ Put your business cards inside your luggage. Tear off all airline tags from

previous trips. Use straps if your bags'
clasps or hinges are weak.

+ Always lock your bags securely—use
  padlocks. Don't rely on flimsy built-in
  locks. For extra security, for an extra
  fee, some airports offer shrinkwrap-
  ping for your luggage.

+ Put brightly colored tape on your bags
  so you can spot them easily as they
  ride by on the carousel. Tie a brightly
  colored ribbon on your suiter bag to
  distinguish it from others.

+ Start your vacation roll with a photo of
  your luggage and its contents, and
  make a list of everything you pack.
  Use it for insurance reimbursement if
  your luggage never arrives.

Captain Wrightway's SHIPPING TRICK

The good captain hates to see nice folks like you lugging things through the airport. Here's a great idea he'd like to share with you:

A day or two before your domestic flight, insure and ship your things by FedEx or UPS to your destination, either overnight or second-day.

Be sure to tell the recipient to expect your package. If it's going to a hotel, write "hold for guest arrival" on the outside and call to alert them it's coming. Take the name of the person you spoke with. Track its progress on the internet. And save the box to ship things back at the end of your trip.

Now, when you get to the airport with only a carry-on, you can skip the long lines at the ticket counter and go through the security checkpoint directly to your gate.

Before you leave

✈ The time you need to arrive at the airport depends on the airline, airport, time of day, season and other factors. Play it safe. Arrive at least:

  • **2 hours** before domestic departures

  • **3 hours** before international flights

✈ Put your photo ID—an up-to-date driver's license or some other valid government-issued proof of identity—into a handy but secure pocket. You'll be pulling it out constantly.

✈ Keep your airline ticket or e-ticket receipt readily available. A valid e-ticket receipt will include your ticket number on it.

✈ All non-U.S. citizens boarding international flights in the United States must show evidence of admission into the U.S., such as a visa, alien resident card, or other approved documentation.

Last-Minute Packing Checklist— Page 141

✈ Do you have your house and luggage keys?

✈ Have you minimized the amount of metal you're carrying and wearing?

✈ Is your talcum powder encapsulated in an airtight bag? Leaking sugar, coffee creamer or any other powder will earn you delays and special attention from security.

✈ Memorize the flight number, departure time, and unique 3-letter airport code for each segment of your journey.

✈ Check the weather at your destination. Pack last-minute items accordingly.

✈ Keep small bills handy for tipping, snacks, luggage carts, etc.

Congratulations! You were right.

The lines ARE long. The hassle is more than it used to be—and that's *a good thing*.

See this for what it is: lines are long because security people really *are* checking more—not automatically waving people through. The delays are proof that new systems are in place, and being respected.

What can you do about it? Use the situation to your advantage. Because you know the checkers will be shuffling through the contents of your bags, treat yourself to that new underwear you've needed for so long (mom would be proud...). Because you know you'll be standing around waiting, indulge in that braincandy paperback you've been eyeing—it'll be easy to carry and a good time-eater. And see any armed guards for who they are: the trained sons and daughters of Americans, dedicated to keeping your flight completely uneventful.

By viewing each so-called hassle as a proof of your increased safety, and using the information like judo to advance your goals, you may actually be able to smile when you get to the head of your line.

At the airport

→ Your vehicle may be searched after you enter the airport. Be prepared to pop open your trunk. Clutter and boxes will slow down the inspection.

→ Check whether the airport allows you to drop off passengers directly in front of your airline's entrance. If you have disabled placards, ask about that.

→ If available, check your bags at curb-side and avoid lines at ticket counters. The convenience is well worth the extra couple-dollar tip per bag.

→ At check-in, be certain they put correct tags on each of your bags—especially any connecting airports. If you don't know the three-letter codes, ask.

→ Make sure they hand you one claim check for each bag you've checked. Hold onto all claim checks until you retrieve your bags and verify that everything's there and undamaged.

✈ Luggage cannot be checked in more than four hours before your departure.

✈ Be aware: the bags you're checking can be searched by security staff at the ticket counter, security checkpoint and/or boarding gate. This is usually done in your presence, and as discreetly as possible.

✈ Every airport announcement may affect you—tune them out at your own risk.

✈ Never agree to carry anything on the plane for another person, especially someone you just met.

✈ Never leave any bag unattended— security will confiscate it.

✈ Some airports offer interdenominational chapels, if you'd be more comfortable checking in with you-know-Who before you fly.

About That Security Checkpoint

Don't be surprised if your nail clippers or underwire bra set off the security scanner —security is adjusting them to be more sensitive than ever before.

Make your trip through the portal as easy as possible: put your keys and change into sandwich-sized zip-seal clear plastic bags. This saves fishing through your pockets before walking through the scanner.

Be ready to walk through immediately after placing your carry-ons on the X-ray belt. You needn't wait for the guard to give you an okay—just walk through, one person at a time, without touching the sides. You may notice you set off scanners in one airport and not another. It's not machine failure—it's how sensitively they're set.

→ If you have a pacemaker or metal implant, notify security personnel in advance. If you have any medical devices that may be questioned, carry your doctor's prescription with you.

→ While you're waiting your turn, remove all metal objects like jewelry, watches, belts, coins and pens and put them in a small plastic bag inside your carry-on.

It's Not About You

Nice people who follow the rules aren't used to being searched, questioned or examined. Now you're standing in line waiting for a stranger to unpack your suitcase and go through your things. You haven't had to be this worried about somebody seeing your underwear since the playground in third grade.

Your gracious cooperation is the contribution you're making to the safety of us all. Thank you.

✈ If you set off the scanner, you may be checked with an electronic wand and patted down by security personnel.

✈ Expect extra checks on laptops, cell phones and other electronics. Remove them from their cases before putting them on the X-ray belt. Be prepared to turn them on to prove what they are.

✈ Diskettes and other magnetic media do not need to be protected from the X-ray machine, but can be ruined by the walk-through scanner. Send them through on the conveyor belt.

✈ Only ticketed passengers are allowed past the screening checkpoint, unless you're a parent or a traveler with a medical reason. Get a 'companion pass' from your airline in advance.

✈ Carrying bottled water or other liquids or foods may slow down your passage. Consider buying them in the concourse beyond the screening area, where food vendors offer well-packaged meals to go.

✈ Once on the other side, reclaim your things as quickly as possible, and try not to block others coming through.

Because airports are full of busy rushing people loaded with luggage, cash and valuables, they make ideal targets for professional thieves and con artists. Here's how NOT to fall prey to their well-tested scams:

The Scanner Scam

While you're emptying your pockets at the scanners, your unattended belongings are ripe for plucking at the other end of the X-ray belt by anyone who acts like the owner. It takes only a second.

Your best defense: Place your bags on the X-ray belt ONLY after you've emptied your pockets into the tray they give you. Try to give yourself clear passage through the scanner so you'll arrive at the other end of the belt before your belongings do.

If you're traveling with a companion, you're in luck. While one of you waits with the carry-ons, the other goes through the scanner. Then you can safely place everything on the belt, knowing who's waiting for it at the other end.

The Distract 'n Grab Scam

Beware of the helpful stranger who points out the fresh splotch of ketchup or other stain on your clothing. Guess how it got there? He or she may be setting you up for a classic "distract-and-grab" scam, with an accomplice. While your attention is diverted, someone else makes off with your unwatched items. Variations of this ruse are endless: a couple suddenly starts an argument right next to you; a stranger asks for directions or change, or speaks to you in a foreign language.

Your best defense: If a stranger approaches you, or you see a suspicious distraction, rely on your sixth sense. It could be nothing—or the beginning of a ruined trip. Keep your things close to you and never take your eyes—or hands—off them. *Any* confusion or distraction is your cue to instantly double your guard.

Now boarding

✈ When you arrive at the gate, check in with the agent—even if you already have a seat assignment.

✈ Don't wander too far from your gate— you may miss your boarding announcement. However, if you have time, make an "insurance trip" to the restroom.

✈ The safest place for purses, briefcases or carry-on bags is between your feet, whether you're standing in line or sitting in the gate area.

✈ If you plan on taking motion medication, do it now so it's in full effect during your flight.

On the plane

If you think the crew's pre-flight announcement is a good time to start a crossword, then you should have no trouble coming up with a seven-letter word for someone who doesn't show good sense.

Sure, you may have heard the safety briefing dozens of times over the years. So let's see you ace the quiz on page 88.

✈ Follow—don't ignore—all instructions given to you by the flight crew. They're for your own safety.

✈ If you are seated in an emergency exit row and don't want the extra responsibilities, request a different seat.

✈ Ask yourself: exactly how many rows am I from each emergency exit? Could I find my way directly to all of them?

✈ Fasten your safety belt snugly around your hips—not your stomach. Keep it fastened even if the captain turns off the seatbelt sign.

✈ Is your carry-on completely under the seat in front of you?

✈ If you feel a draft—or if you're too warm—you can always adjust the airflow nozzle over your head. Cabin temperature will stabilize once you're airborne. If you need a blanket, ask the flight attendant.

✈ Take a moment now to familiarize yourself with the operation of your safety belt, life vest and oxygen mask. Read the safety card in the seat pocket in front of you. If you have questions, ask.

✈ Your access to the lavatory may be restricted during flight, or blocked by the cart during beverage and meal service. Plan your trips accordingly.

✈ Boy, were you smart to bring something to read!

You think YOUR job is tough?

How would you like to juggle inventory and organize schedules? Placate screaming toddlers, calm frightened folks and subdue belligerent drunks? Handle medical emergencies, the range of human emotions and hot liquids? And even make correct change.

So—how are YOU making your flight attendant's job easier?

✈ Smile! This is someone also away from home, whose family is doing something else right now. Be friendly. 'Please' and 'thank you' go a long way.

✈ Turn off your cell phone or laptop when you're asked. You're delaying everyone.

✈ Unless you're in real personal discomfort, stay in your seat while the beverage cart is in the aisle.

✈ Don't grab hot drinks. Wait till they're handed to you.

✈ If YOU can't hoist your carry-on, don't expect a flight attendant to put it in the overhead bin for you.

Captain Wrightway's

Official On-Board Etiquette Guide

→ Slamming your seat back could give someone behind you a hot coffee surprise.

→ Slamming your tray-table closed could give someone in front of you a real pain in the neck.

→ To avoid the evil eye from everyone, shut your window shade during the movie.

→ If you're going for "frequent tinkler miles," book an aisle seat.

→ Keep your stuff under the seat in front of you. Constant jumping up to open the overhead bin could earn you a salted nuts shower from fellow flyers.

→ Use the phone softly. No one wants to hear details of Aunt Edna's operation.

→ Hand your trash to the flight attendants when they come asking for it. You don't get prizes for finding clever new places to hide it.

→ Wait for the announcement before opening overstuffed overhead bins. The head you save may be your own.

Captain Wrightway's SAFETY QUIZ

Just when you think it's safe to snooze, here comes that pre-flight safety demo. You've heard it so often, you think you can recite it in your sleep. Well let's just see, shall we?

Circle True or False:

1. **T or F**   Not all planes have the oxygen mask located in the overhead compartment.

2. **T or F**   If you're traveling with a child, place the oxygen mask over your own mouth first, and *then* tend to the child's mask.

3. **T or F**   Emergency exit doors may operate differently, depending on the type of aircraft.

4. **T or F**   Flotation devices are inflated by using the bicycle pump located under the armrest.

5. **T or F**   Floor lights along the aisles will guide you to all emergency exits.

Answers on page 157

Upon landing

✈ Pay attention to all announcements, and stay seated with your seatbelt fastened until the sign is turned off.

✈ Set your watch to local time.

✈ Check to ensure you have all of your belongings.

✈ If you have a connecting flight, listen for connecting gate information. If you don't hear it, ask when you reach the gate area.

✈ Follow the signs to baggage claim and ground transportation.

Reuniting with your luggage

✈ Be careful not to walk off with bags that *look* like yours. Check the luggage tags.

✈ If you don't see your bags when the carousel stops, go to the baggage claim office, usually nearby.

- ✈ If your bags aren't there, fill out the missing luggage form, *even if they say your luggage should arrive on the next flight*. Keep a copy of the form, and write down your claim check numbers, the agent's name and a *direct* phone number.

- ✈ Until your bags are found, some airlines provide you with emergency toiletries or other essentials—ask. Others will reimburse you for reasonable expenses. Hold onto your receipts.

- ✈ If your checked luggage or its contents are lost, damaged or stolen, you are entitled to compensation. The small print on your ticket spells out money limits, and which items are not covered.

✈ If your bag is damaged, torn or open, check immediately to see if any items are missing. Fill out the paperwork *before* you leave the airport. Get a copy of the form, the agent's name and a *direct* phone number.

✈ If you discover later that items are missing, call the airline immediately. Take notes on the who/what/when/where of your call. Follow up with a certified letter.

✈ If your bag is lost, you'll have to negotiate with the airline for the amount of compensation. For more information, or if you are dissatisfied with their offer, see page 152.

✈ Don't panic. Many bags are found within 2 to 48 hours, and the airline will usually deliver them to wherever you're staying.

The Clouds Below

One of the most exhilarating experiences is to take off on a dark, rainy day and within a few minutes be flying through bright sunshine and blue skies. Soaring above the clouds gives you the thrill of watching the weather at work, safely, like no TV newscaster can show you. Clouds are big clues to the weather...if you can read them.

Essentially, clouds are nothing more than tiny ice crystals and fine water droplets. They're formed by movements of air and by changes in temperature and altitude. We can't see through them, but a pilot's instruments can.

Clouds come in all shapes and sizes, but actually fall into several categories, which make them easy to identify.

Cirrus

Cirrus clouds are highest, appearing as feathery white streaks in the cold air above 20,000 feet. They're made entirely of ice crystals carried along by winds of varying speeds. When a faster wind picks up the main part of the cloud, some of the remaining ice crystals trail behind, forming what are commonly called "mares' tails."

Stratus

Stratus clouds form in layers or sheets, and are made of tiny water droplets. From the ground, you see stratus clouds as a familiar low-hanging gray ceiling, often accompanied by fog or drizzle. As your plane climbs, you may also see stratus clouds at higher levels, called altostratus and cirrostratus, indicating stable air masses. Above these clouds, you'll only get rare glimpses of the ground; but don't worry, it's still there.

Cumulus

Cumulus clouds are big, white and fluffy. Joni Mitchell celebrated them as "ice-cream castles in the air." They occur in rising warm air; in small groups they indicate fair weather. If you're flying over the ocean in a clear blue sky, look for small puffs in the distance. It probably means there are islands below them.

Cumulus clouds can grow to dramatic proportions several thousand feet high and are beautiful to behold. You usually see them from the side because pilots will fly around them.

Why Is The Sky Blue?

It depends on who's asking.

If it's YOU, here's the scoop: Sunlight is actually a combination of all colors of the spectrum, each one traveling on a different wavelength. When light reaches the earth's atmosphere, the invisible air molecules scatter only the shorter blue and violet rays, and let the others pass through. This infinite scattering fills the sky with continuous blue light.

When skies are gray, it's because larger particles in the air are scattering more wavelengths from the spectrum. Water droplets in clouds scatter all wavelengths, making the clouds appear white. Pollution particles are the right size to create yellow or brownish colors. Sunsets are fiery red because only the longer red and orange wavelengths can escape through the dense lower atmosphere to light up the sky.

And if it's your KID who's asking, the answer is, "Just because."

Free Light Shows

Flying high above the weather gives you a clear advantage over ground-bound folks to see a few of nature's spectacular light phenomena.

Round rainbows

At ground-level, your view is limited, so you can only see the part of a rainbow that arcs to somewhere over the horizon. But from the air, you can see the entire rainbow in its dazzling full-circle display!

Glowing glories

As you fly above layers of clouds, try to spot the plane's shadow on them. If conditions are right, you'll witness a "glory"—a circle of colored light around the shadow. Sometimes you'll see only the glory, if the plane is too high to cast a shadow. You're not likely to see a glory at ground level, but watch for them from your window seat.

Clues In The Landscape

The changing scenery on the ground is part science, part modern art and part poetry—a testament to both natural forces and human ingenuity. And just like a walk through a museum, if you don't know what you're looking at, you'll miss the richness of the experience.

For starters, look in the back of your in-flight magazine for the airline route map and trace your own flight path. A good map will show topographical features, like the mountains and plains you'll cross.

You can tell the relative ages of mountains by their features. High mountains with sharp, jagged edges are the youngsters—from 70 to 250 million years old—the tough erosion forces of wind, water and ice haven't worn them down. When you're crossing the western two-thirds of the U.S., study the Rockies and the Sierra Nevada.

You want old? Check out the Appalach-
ians, stretching from Maine to Alabama.
See how 600 million years of erosion have
turned the Berkshires, Adirondacks and
Blue Ridge Mountains into soft, rounded,
tree-covered humps.

Many rivers show up as long silver ribbons
threading through the landscape. You may
first spot the tell-tale clumps of trees that
line most river banks before you even
catch a glimpse of a river. Follow them to
see where the river runs.

You can tell if a river is old by looking for
large loops in its course, like the Mississippi River below St. Louis. A younger
river, like the Columbia between Washington and Oregon, tends to run straight.

The human footprint. The vast
checkerboard of the Great Plains and
Midwest was created by ownership
boundaries and various farming methods.
In the semi-arid climate of Kansas and
Nebraska, bright green circles watered by
center-pivot irrigation systems stand out
in a brown and golden quilt. And here,
rows of trees separating fields do not
indicate river banks; rather they shield

loose soil from relentless winds.

Leaving the Midwest, look for the crooked and seemingly haphazard patchwork of land east of the Mississippi River. This reflects the Old World system of property division, where each parcel of land was allowed to border at least part of a stream.

Roads also provide clues to the terrain. Straight lines indicate level ground, while twists and turns follow the contours of land with varying elevations.

Cities located on coastlines and major waterways give away their old age. More recent cities developed inland as rail and highway hubs reflect the nation's rich transportation history.

Why Planes Fly 101

If we learned the secrets of flight from the birds, then how on earth does a plane get off the ground without flapping its wings?

Early inventors kept trying to copy the only model of flying they knew—and kept falling flat—until they discovered that two forces are involved in flying, lift and thrust, and were able to harness each force separately.

Lift. You've already experienced lift first-hand when you've put your arm outside the window of a moving car. By holding your fingers together pointed into the wind, and tilting your palm up slightly, you felt an upward pull created by suction along the back of your hand. That's lift. Amazingly, you can get the same result by simply arching your palm. And if you try both tilting and arching together, you'll understand how the shape of a wing lifts the plane. (Try this at home, not on the plane!) Actual lift is determined by the wing's size, angle of tilt and the speed of

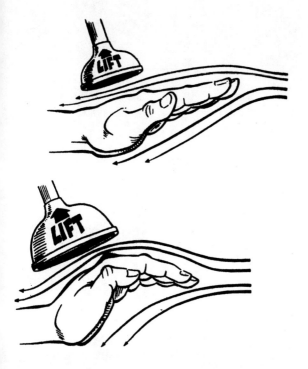

CROSS SECTION
OF WING

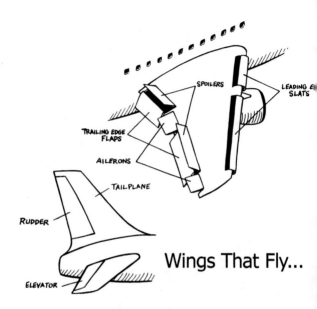

SPOILERS

LEADING E
SLATS

TRAILING EDGE
FLAPS

AILERONS

TAILPLANE

RUDDER

ELEVATOR

Wings That Fly...

the plane. And any object can be carried in the air, regardless of size or weight, if it's equipped with the right-sized wings.

Thrust. While lift acts to counter the plane's weight, thrust is the forward propulsion needed to overcome the "drag" caused by the plane's resistance to the air. In birds, thrust comes from flapping their wings; in planes, it's produced by power from propellers or jet engines.

Controlling Flight. The key to smooth flying is controlling thrust and lift together. Pilots do this by adjusting the flaps, slats and spoilers on the wings during take-off, landing and for steering. The best seats for seeing these carefully orchestrated movements are from the rear third of the plane.

Wings are also designed to flex up and down during flight, offering smoother rides. It's a safety feature, and it's perfectly normal. And if you see liquid streaming across the wings in flight, don't worry. Water vapor often condenses on the top side of the wings, especially on humid days.

...And Wings That Don't

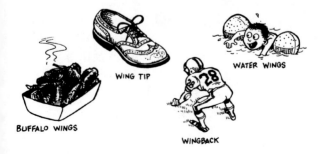

BUFFALO WINGS

WING TIP

WATER WINGS

WINGBACK

Gee!-Force

As the plane accelerates on takeoff, you will feel slightly heavier and pushed back into your seat. No, it's not what you ate. It's the acceleration force— or G-force.

Don't worry. It's the same feeling you get in your car or a fast-rising elevator. If it seems odd to you, imagine what the space shuttle astronauts must experience during a launch. You'll also feel slightly more G-force when the pilot changes direction on banked turns.

No astronaut experience would be complete without weightlessness, and at some point during the flight—as the plane quickly levels off right after takeoff, or on descent—you may suddenly feel a little lighter in your seat. It's that fast-moving elevator again, this time going back to the lobby. Enjoy it. You'll never lose weight more easily.

Headwinds Or Tailwinds?

If you've ever headed into a strong wind with an open umbrella, you can appreciate the job the plane has to do. Every ten miles-per-hour of headwind adds ten miles to the distance the plane must fly every hour. On the other hand, tailwinds go in the same direction as the plane, helping to carry it along faster and save fuel. The airlines build these factors into their schedules.

Turbulence is simply air that isn't smooth. It usually feels like riding over a bumpy street in a bus. Pilots can tell where turbulence occurs and try to steer clear of it. If they do go through it, stay calm. They'll tell you to keep your seatbelt fastened while they head toward smoother air.

Name That Noise

The normal sounds of air travel.

Clomp! Thunk! Whir-r-r! What the heck was that? Don't worry. Those are just some of the harmless noises you hear on takeoff, landing and occasionally during flight. Here's what causes some of them:

➤ Luggage being loaded into the belly of the plane *whumps* and *thuds* beneath the floor.

➤ Air conditioning units may also vibrate and *hummm* under your feet.

➤ The covered ramp connecting the terminal to the plane *whirrs* away from the door.

• New brake pads can *grind* during taxiing or landing.

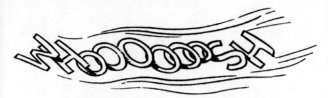

+ Landing wheels *clomp* as they lock into position, and *thunk* when retracted back into their housings. You may also hear the housing doors *clank* shut.

+ If the engines get louder on takeoff— and then immediately softer—that's okay. Pilots do that to reduce noise as they fly over residential areas.

+ The angles of the wing flaps and slats are deliberately adjusted during takeoffs and landings. You may hear them *flick* or *whirr* into place.

+ The air nozzle over your seat may *hiss*. If it bugs you, reach up and screw it shut.

CLOMP!

+ Normal landings include *thumps*, *screeches* from the wheels, *whines* from the flaps, and a *long loud roar* as the engines slow the plane down.

Meet Chuck!

In the seatpocket in front of you dwells an ornery and lonely genie whom people often treat poorly. This is your chance to become his friend.

Just fish him out of the pocket and draw in the face on the next page. Then tear out the holes as shown on this diagram. Now he's ready to meet and entertain everyone around you, and maybe he'll even reward each of them with three wishes. Kids love him!

NOTE: DURING TURBULENCE, DO NOT DISTURB CHUCK.

Guarantee:
All dialogue spoken to
airline reservation agents.

✈ A man calls an airline's 800-number from a pay phone at the airport, looks over at ticket counter and shouts, "Which one of you am I talking to? Raise your hand."

✈ A woman is told she'll have to make one change between Newark and Los Angeles. She demands to know why she'll need to change clothes.

✈ A woman actually says, "My kitchen" when asked where she's calling from.

✈ A man asks if his flight stops at Exit 7A on the New Jersey Turnpike.

✈ A twenty-something calls to complain that the flight was "bumpy" and the peanuts were "stale."

✈ A caller asks for a morning flight that leaves "around 7 p.m."

✈ Another caller inquires, "Today is the 19th. If I leave tomorrow, what day will that be?"

✈ After the agent confirms a lengthy reservation and repeats all the flight information, the caller says, "Maybe I should write this down."

Things That Make Flight Attendants Crabby

Or what NOT to do
to get good service.

Your flight attendant is a professional trained to handle many emergencies, most of which you'll never see. Here are some things inconsiderate people do to drive them batty. Don't do this stuff!

✈ Ring the call button for magazines during meal service.

✈ Ask them to repeat the whole list of drinks—twice.

✈ Shove aside the aisle cart to get to the lavatory.

✈ Mistake the service galley for a lavatory.

✈ Hand them a used diaper.

✈ Engage in a lengthy debate with yourself when they ask what you'd like to drink.

✈ Ask if a lavatory is vacant when the OCCUPIED sign is on.

✈ Make passes at them. From the window seat.

✈ Growl at them for flight delays.

✈ Don't return smiles or say "thank you."

Things That Make YOU Crabby

Just as you settle down in your seat for a long flight, someone invariably does something to irritate. Here are the top passenger peeves from a recent survey.

- ✈ Snoring seatmates on your right.
- ✈ Airsick seatmates on your left.
- ✈ Seat-back recliners in front of you.
- ✈ Kicking screaming brats behind you.
- ✈ Hair spritzers who miss.
- ✈ Hyperactive kids...with passive parents.
- ✈ Gabbers, while you're trying to sleep.
- ✈ Sleepers, when you're trying to gab.
- ✈ Ignorant know-it-alls.
- ✈ Armrest hoggers.
- ✈ Cheap cologne from ten rows back.
- ✈ Overpowering BO right next to you.
- ✈ Overhead bin storage hogs.
- ✈ Middle-seat diaper-changers.
- ✈ Overactive bladders in window seats.
- ✈ Clipped fingers from the beverage cart in the aisle seat.
- ✈ Window shades wide open during the movie.
- ✈ Add yours: _____

Surefire Conversation Starters

Fill in your own.
Then hold this page up to the
person sitting next to you.

Don't

✈ *"Whooh!* I never shoulda ate all those airport chili dogs."

✈ "Wanna see my rash?"

✈ *"Zip-feh neggle-boo flok?"*

✈ "I have proof our elected leaders are actually Nexus warriors from Alpha Centauri."

✈ "Do you know about the great franchise opportunities in worm farming?"

✈ "Can I borrow your Chapstick?"

✈ "That Carrot Top is REALLY funny!"

✈ "Did you get a body cavity search, too?"

✈ "Where I come from, even the sacred goats do not eat this good."

✈ "Can you get me that...little...bag...in...front.....of...you?"

Do

✈ A warm smile. A friendly hello.

Guarantee:
All events witnessed by
flight attendants.

✈ Upon entering a plane, a woman is told she has a window seat. "I can't sit there," she exclaims "I just had my hair done."

✈ New parents are told their babyseat must go in the overhead bin. Later, the flight attendant sees it has indeed been stowed—with the baby still in it.

✈ A man is observed trying to order a drink by talking directly into the overhead PA system, "like the drive-thru at Jack-In-The-Box," said the flight attendant.

✈ A businessman tries to board a with an oversized carry-on bag. Since the plane is full, the flight attendant asks him to check it. Indignantly, the man thunders, "Lady, do you know who I am?" The flight attendant immediately turns to the planeload of passengers and says, "Excuse me, ladies and gentlemen. This man has forgotten who he is. Does anyone know him?"

✈ A flight attendant is crawling around on her hands and knees, obviously looking for something. When asked what she's looking for, without missing a beat, she replies, "I'm looking for the glamour they promised me with this job."

The Miraculous International Child Shusher™

Is some little monster screaming, running around or kicking the back of your seat? If you've tried every polite gesture—from throat-clearing to intense glaring—now's the time to flip this page to the parents.

If that doesn't work, hold up the next two pages and see which one does!

CURB YOUR KID!

P·l·e·a·s·e!

Halten Sie bitte Ihr Kind zurück!

¡Frene su niño, por favor!

Réprimez votre enfant, s'il vous plaît!

Trattenga il Suo bambino, per favore!

Someone Special In The Air

Smart flying ideas
for special travelers

Flying Kids

Kids on planes cry, run, holler, fight and spill. Weary flight attendants mutter that some kids do everything but sleep. You can make your child's flight happier for both of you.

In advance

✈ Children under two usually fly free on domestic flights if they sit on your lap. It's safest to secure them in safety seats, and some airlines let you reserve the seat next to you at a discount. Children over age two pay full fare in most cases. Ask your airline—child safety rules may be evolving.

✈ Be prepared to show your child's birth certificate to qualify for fare discounts and free flights. Children flying free do not qualify for any baggage allowance.

✈ If you plan to use your regular carseat on the plane, make sure it has an FAA-approved label on it. Otherwise, you'll have to check it as luggage.

✈ Request seats in the bulkhead—the first seats in any section of the plane—where there's more floor space, and you may be closer to the restrooms.

✈ Give yourself an extra half hour more than other travelers are advised. Remember, your child will need to be fed and distracted during this extra waiting time.

✈ Airlines' kid amenities differ. Ask about special kids' meals, airport activity rooms and on-board entertainment kits.

✈ Does you child have ear problems? Talk to your pediatrician before flying.

Day of the flight

✈ Dress both of you for comfort. Carry extra diapers, and a change of clothes for each of you, in case unexpected things come up.

✈ Create a busy bag with non-messy snacks, simple toys, crayons and a few surprises—but no scissors. Include water, juice boxes, a sweater and any important medication—enough to sustain your child in case of a 24-hour luggage delay. Pack favorite toys—but no toy guns or plastic swords.

✈ Time a small snack before scheduled departure so your child won't be too hungry to accept a bottle on takeoff.

✈ At the gate, always ask for pre-boarding privileges. Use the extra quiet time to get settled.

On the plane

✈ Babies and small children cry on take-off and landing because of air pressure changes that hurt their ears. This is the time to start a bottle, get out the pacifier, or hand out chewing gum.

✈ Never hand a dirty diaper to the flight attendant. Seal it in an airsickness bag; if you can, dispose of it in the proper lavatory trash bin.

✈ Some aircraft now offer convenient fold-

down changing tables in at least one
lavatory. Ask.

✈ Be safe and considerate—control your
   kid. The aisle is not a playground, and
   your child could get hurt.

✈ If you can't mute the sounds on their
   handheld electronic games—leave the
   games at home.

Upon arrival

✈ The baggage carousel looks like a fun
   carnival ride, but it's dangerous. Keep
   kids away!

✈ Spring for the extra bucks—rent a
   luggage cart. Make your life easier.
   Your toddler can ride and so can your
   bags.

Unaccompanied Children

Airlines transport kids traveling by themselves every year. It can be scarier for parents than for kids; but if it's necessary for your child to fly alone, do it right:

In advance

✈ Tell the airline your child will be traveling alone and ask about age requirements, fees, assistance, and special forms you'll need to fill out. Ask about any recent changes to their UM (unaccompanied minor) program.

✈ Most airlines will only book your child on a non-stop flight, so you don't have to worry about missed connections along the way.

✈ Get a 'companion pass' from your airline so you will be allowed to accompany your child through security to the gate. Request another pass so your child can be greeted at the arrival gate.

Day of the flight

✈ Make three copies of your child's identification and flight plans, plus your

own information, including your cell
phone number; and the name,
address, home and cell phone
numbers of the person meeting her.
Place a copy in her carry-on bag, in
her luggage and on her person, along
with some cash and coins for the
phone.

✈ Arrive early to fill out forms.

✈ Introduce your child to the flight crew.

✈ Stay at the gate till the plane takes off.

Upon arrival

✈ The person
meeting your
child should
arrive at the
airport early—
prepared to
show photo ID
that precisely
matches the
name you
supplied on
the airline
form.

Dealing With OPAKs

(Other People's Annoying Kids)

You can't shut 'em up or hypnotize 'em, but you *can* divert 'em. Here's how:

✈ Carry a few inexpensive child-safe plastic toys to give to aggravating kids.

✈ Give 'em the comics from your paper. It's cheap self-defense.

✈ Be sure to ask the parent first—kids should be properly taught not to accept goodies from strangers.

Grown-Ups

✈ Register with a friend: give someone your itinerary, phone numbers where you can be reached, and when you're due back.

✈ Lighten your wallet or purse before you go. Take out the library card, unnecessary membership and department store credit cards, office pass-keys, etc. But be sure to leave in your valid photo ID and auto club card—even if you don't plan to drive.

✈ Don't miss the opportunity to ask seat-mates for tips about your destination city, such as good restaurants, shortcuts from the airport, the must-sees and the must-avoids.

✈ If you don't want to talk to your seat-mate, wear headphones. You don't even need a tape player—just tuck the plug into a pocket.

✈ For fewer distractions, avoid sitting in or near the bulkhead—especially at holidays, or from May through September. That's where unescorted children or families with kids usually sit.

✈ Don't start a game or a conversation with an unescorted child, unless you want to play surrogate parent for the rest of the flight.

Savvy women

✈ Don't wear your good jewelry—you'll be an obvious target for thieves. Leave the good stuff at home.

✈ Walk with a sense of purpose: a little tough, not one to be bothered.

✈ Bring only as much as you can carry comfortably—luggage on wheels helps. Being overladen makes you vulnerable.

✈ When sitting, your carry-on bag is safest when it's wedged between your feet. If there's room, put your purse in your carry-on bag.

✈ Married or not, consider wearing a wedding ring. It may not repel hard-core wolves, but it sends a message that you're not to be bothered.

✈ Memorize a few phrases in some obscure language. Unwelcome strangers can be told, "Garbage in season is riper at home" in Phoenician. Stops 'em cold.

✈ At check-in, you can ask to be seated next to another female passenger.

✈ In public restrooms, don't hang your purse on the hooks inside the door. A thief can lift it from over the door, and you're in no position to give chase.

✈ Pregnant women should check with their doctor and the airline about potential restrictions. Pack healthy snacks, and book an aisle seat for easy lavatory access.

Travelers With Disabilities

Airlines in the U.S. are required to accommodate most everyone with a disability. To help ensure a smooth flight, discuss your needs in advance with your travel agent and airline.

✈ Call your airline, local airport—and all connecting airports—to assist with any special needs, such as a wheelchair.

✈ If you're bringing an electric wheelchair, the battery must say 'Gel Cell' or it will need to be disconnected and removed.

✈ If you're carrying an oxygen tank, it must be empty. Request on-board oxygen from your airline, and call each airport (including stop-overs) for tanks to be brought to you on the ground.

✈ If you are not accommodated like any other passenger, ask to speak to the Complaint Resolution Officer immediately to help resolve your problem.

✈ Visit *www.sath.org* for more information

Your Last-Minute Flight Check

You won't need *everything* from home —just the good stuff. Check off the things you need to remember—or pick up whatever you forget at a local pharmacy.

Must-Haves

- ☐ Passport/visa/citizenship proof
- ☐ Approved photo ID
- ☐ Airline tickets/E-ticket receipts
- ☐ Travel itinerary
- ☐ "In Case Of Emergency" contact info
- ☐ Airline VIP/frequent flyer cards
- ☐ Hotel/car/transportation reservations
- ☐ Health & vaccination documentation
- ☐ Cash, travelers checks, credit cards, ATM card
- ☐ Small bills for tipping
- ☐ Trip cancellation/medical insurance
- ☐ Medical alert card, tag or bracelet
- ☐ Medical insurance card
- ☐ Phone numbers of trusted neighbor, family member, physician, dentist, optician and insurance agent
- ☐ Security wallet or moneybelt
- ☐ Luggage keys
- ☐ Small flashlight
- ☐ _____
- ☐ _____

Essentials

- ☐ Guidebooks and maps of where you're going
- ☐ Bottled water
- ☐ Pocket compass
- ☐ Comfortable old walking shoes
- ☐ Sunglasses, extra eyeglasses, reading glasses, spare contacts
- ☐ Wouldn't-hurt-to-lose-it watch
- ☐ Folding umbrella/raincoat/poncho
- ☐ Conversion tables: metric, money, etc.
- ☐ Notebook and dependable pen
- ☐ Electric/phone adapters & chargers
- ☐ Camera, film and lead-lined bag
- ☐ Business cards
- ☐ Batteries: camera, flashlight, calculator, hearing aid, videocamera

Would Be Nice

- ☐ Videocamera and tapes
- ☐ Personal stereo and music
- ☐ Ear plugs
- ☐ Binoculars
- ☐ Hunting/fishing licenses

Captain Wrightway's CARRY-ON OR NOT?

Never Carry

✈ Knives and cutting instruments of any kind, length or composition, including spare blades

✈ Corkscrews, ice picks, straight razors, metal scissors and nail files

✈ Golf clubs, baseball bats, pool cues, hockey sticks, ski poles

Okay To Carry (may be inspected)

✈ Walking cane & umbrella

✈ Nail clipper/tweezer/ eyelash curler

✈ Safety & disposable razors

✈ Syringes (carry documented proof of medical need and accompanying medicine in original container)

For all connecting luggage and carry-on information: *www.helpmefly.net*

Will You Be Sorry If You Don't Have..?

- ☐ Chewing gum for ear-pressure relief
- ☐ Sleeping pills
- ☐ Motion-sickness remedy
- ☐ Spare contact lenses & solutions
- ☐ Visor/brimmed hat
- ☐ Swimsuit
- ☐ Scarf
- ☐ Vitamins
- ☐ Foam shoe insoles
- ☐ Bathroom tissue
- ☐ Travel hair drier
- ☐ Travel iron
- ☐ Travel shoeshine kit/plastic shoehorn
- ☐ Sleep shades/neck pillow/ear plugs
- ☐ Portable hotel door lock
- ☐ Small first aid kit
- ☐ Extra set of luggage keys
- ☐ Kid's busy bag
- ☐ Extension cord
- ☐ Book to read

Will You Feel More Secure With..?

- ☐ All personal prescriptions
- ☐ Antacids/heartburn medication
- ☐ Hand sanitizer/towelettes
- ☐ Sunscreen
- ☐ Eye drops
- ☐ Diarrhea remedy
- ☐ Laxative/fiber therapy
- ☐ Cold/flu remedy
- ☐ Small lint brush
- ☐ Adhesive tape & bandages
- ☐ Antiseptic ointment
- ☐ Dandruff remedy
- ☐ Bug repellent
- ☐ Bug-bite ointment
- ☐ Nasal spray/antihistamines
- ☐ Condoms
- ☐ Water purification tablets

Packing Hint. Pack shampoos, cosmetics, floppy disks—anything that needs encapsulating —into quart-sized zipper-seal bags or unbreakable containers. It'll keep 'em from leaking all over your clothing.

Personal Stuff

You know what you need—slip this stuff in with it. Tighten screw-tops so nothing oozes. Zipper-lock bags are a blessing. Carry on what you can't live without.

- ☐ Travel alarm clock
- ☐ Cotton swabs
- ☐ Styptic pencil
- ☐ Moisturizer
- ☐ Lip balm
- ☐ Toothpaste, brush, floss
- ☐ Comb, hairbrush
- ☐ Shampoo, conditioner
- ☐ Deodorant
- ☐ Cosmetics
- ☐ Perfume/cologne/aftershave
- ☐ Disposable toilet seat covers
- ☐ Tampons/sanitary protection
- ☐ Cold-water fabric wash
- ☐ Sink stopper
- ☐ Individual moist towelettes
- ☐ Tissues
- ☐ Dragon-mouth killers

Most Predicaments
Can Be Fixed With...

- ☐ Aspirin/ibuprofen/Tylenol
- ☐ Clear nail polish
- ☐ Duct tape
- ☐ Crazy Glue
- ☐ Foreign language phrase book/translator

Did You Make Photocopies?
Guard these like real documents.

- ☐ Airline tickets, all pages
- ☐ E-ticket receipts
- ☐ Passport, visa
- ☐ Travel itinerary
- ☐ Travelers check numbers & refund instructions
- ☐ Confirmations for all reservations: plane, car, hotel, special events, etc.
- ☐ All credit cards, fronts and backs
- ☐ Travel insurance documentation
- ☐ Personal address book
- ☐ Your eyeglass prescription
- ☐ Personal medical summary
- ☐ Medical and auto insurance cards

Other Stuff I Need To Bring...

You know what you need. Jot it down now while you're thinking about it.

☐ _____

☐ _____

☐ _____

☐ _____

☐ _____

☐ _____

☐ _____

☐ _____

☐ _____

☐ _____

☐ _____

☐ _____

Captain Wrightway's
MONEY SAFE

**Your money is for things YOU want—
don't lose it because of what some
stranger wants.**

✈ Write down the serial numbers of
your travelers checks together
with the phone number to call for
replacements. Always keep this
separate from the checks.

✈ Carry travelers checks separate
from your passport and other ID.
Stolen checks may be passed
without question when backed up
by another form of ID.

✈ If you carry a checkbook, put in a
new register pad before leaving
home. Why reveal your hefty bank
balance to prying eyes every time
you write a check?

✈ Security wallets and moneybelts
come in all shapes and sizes.
Wear one—and disappoint a
pickpocket.

Of course you'll never
need this—but if you do:

FBI (202) 324-3000

Or call **911** from anywhere
in the United States.

Complaint Department

Passengers rarely know their rights when they feel they've been wronged. And Uncle Sam usually doesn't get involved in consumer disputes that go beyond lost luggage, overbooking and delays or cancellations on domestic flights—which are covered by specific rules. Beyond that, it's up to the airline.

For you, it comes down to two things: 1) Speak up. 2) Negotiate.

Airline customer service reps can usually answer your questions about their compensation policies. Also, refer to the fine print on your ticket. If you can read legalese, request a copy of the Conditions of Carriage.

Try to take care of any problem immediately. Speak up pleasantly and clearly to the airline's representative—or that person's supervisor. Try to be reasonable, especially if they're dealing with a whole planeload of problems at the same time.

If that doesn't work, take notes and take names. When you get home, take it up with the consumer relations department at the airline's headquarters. If you used a travel agency, get it involved. And if you are unable to get satisfaction directly with the airline, you may want to appeal to a higher authority.

Consumer Issues: DOT

For information or action about lost or damaged baggage, overbooking, delayed or cancelled flights or other consumer issues regarding a U.S. or foreign airline, the Department of Transportation's

Consumer Affairs Division can advise you of your rights under federal law and act as mediator with the airline.

Call: (202) 366-2220
Visit: *www.dot.gov/airconsumer/problems.htm*
Write: USDOT, C-75, Room 4107, Washington D.C. 20590

When putting your complaint in writing, include your name, address, daytime phone number and a photocopy of your airline ticket, if possible. Be clear, to the point, and keep a copy of your letter.

Safety Issues: FAA

For action on complaints involving carry-on bags, airport security, child safety seats, hazardous materials, malfunctioning aircraft equipment or air-traffic procedures, contact the Federal Aviation Administration.

Call: 1-800-FAA-SURE
Visit: *www.faa.gov*
Write: FAA Consumer Hotline, AOA-20 800 Independence Avenue, SW, Washington, DC 20591

More consumer assistance

✈ **American Society of Travel Agents** may help mediate your complaint against a travel agency, airline, hotel or travel supplier.

Call: (703) 739-8739
Visit: *www.astanet.com*
Write: ASTA Consumer Affairs, 1101 King Street, Suite 200, Alexandria, VA 22314

✈ **PassengerRights.com** will help you lodge complaints with airlines and federal officials.

Visit: *www.passengerrights.com*

✈ **TravelProblems.com** will attempt to negotiate a settlement on your behalf for a fee. If they're unable to reach a settlement you agree to, they say they'll refund your fee.

Visit: *www.travelproblems.com*

✈ **Better Business Bureau** will let you file your complaint online, and forward it to the appropriate local Better Business Bureau based on the ZIP code of the company involved in your dispute.

Visit: *www.bbb.org*

Folks I'd LOVE to see

if only they'd fly!

Uniquely lovable
Aunt Edna

1 _____

2 _____

3 _____

My new
internet pal

Proud new
parents

4 _____

5 _____

6 _____

Complete your list.
Then send each one a
fresh copy of this book!
Easy: *helpmefly.net*

Mr. Right

Suggestion Box

Whether you're a road warrior or a first-time flyer, we'd love to hear your ideas for safer travel. Your tips could earn you a free book!

Send your feedback directly to the author: *natalie@helpmefly.net* Thanks!

Captain Wrightway's ANSWER KEY

No cheating on the Safety Quiz! Turn to page 88 and start with the QUESTIONS!

Questions 1, 2, 3, 5 — C'mon, you know they're all true!

Question 4 — False *—see me after the flight...*

Visit **helpmefly.net**

✈ Latest news, travel links and flying reassurances.

✈ Where to send your tips and suggestions for the next edition.

✈ How to get copies of this book for yourself, your friends—or in quantity for your organization.

As You Fly Home

The only thing better than jetting off to adventures is flying safely home. Your trip isn't just for you and Aunt Dorothy. You're also doing good for everyone who depends on you, an industry that needs your business, and the entire American economy.

Most important, you're showing we will continue to be the best of what we are: brave, unthreatened and resolute in carrying on what matters.

Good for you, and good for us!

Glad we did
this together!